27

W9-CCY-002

U.S. ARMED FORCES

The U.S. COAST GUARD

MICHAEL BENSON

LERNER PUBLICATIONS COMPANY / MINNEAPOLIS

CHAPTER OPENER PHOTO CAPTIONS *J 359.97 Benson*

Cover: A U.S. Coast Guard security boat patrols Boston Harbor in Massachusetts.

Ch. 1: A Coast Guard rescue team races to the scene of the World Trade Center attack on September 11, 2001.

Ch. 2: New recruits receive final orders before boarding the Coast Guard cutter *Eagle* for five weeks of basic training.

Ch. 3: Cadets and crew members aboard the Coast Guard cutter *Eagle* set the sails during training.

Ch. 4: A Coast Guard vessel splashes through stormy ocean waves.

To Larry Beck, Ed Behringer, Scott Frommer, and Anthony Conigliaro

The author wishes to thank the following individuals and organizations: Domenica Di Piazza; Jake Elwell; Peg Goldstein; Second Class Petty Officer Mike Hvozda; the National Baseball Library, Cooperstown, New York; and Steve Blando, Community Relations Branch, U.S. Coast Guard Public Affairs.

Lerner Publications Company
A division of Lerner Publishing Group
241 First Avenue North
Minneapolis, MN 55401 U.S.A.

Website address: www.lernerbooks.com

Library of Congress Cataloging-in-Publication Data

Benson, Michael.
    The U.S. Coast Guard / by Michael Benson.
       p.   cm. — (U.S. Armed Forces)
    Includes bibliographical references and index.
    ISBN: 0-8225-1647-0 (lib. bdg. : alk. paper)
    1. United States. Coast Guard—Juvenile literature.   I. Title.   II. Series: U.S. Armed
Forces (Series : Lerner Publications)
    VG53.B45 2005
    363.28'6'0973—dc22   2004003006

Manufactured in the United States of America
1 2 3 4 5 6 – JR – 10 09 08 07 06 05

CONTENTS

chapter ONE

HISTORY

SEPTEMBER 11, 2001, will always be remembered as one of the worst days in U.S. history. On that day, a group of terrorists hijacked four airplanes. The terrorists flew two of the planes into the two World Trade Center towers in New York City. The buildings collapsed, and thousands of people died. Another plane hit the Pentagon near Washington, D.C. The fourth crashed in Pennsylvania.

Immediately, the U.S. Coast Guard went into action. The Coast Guard is in charge of protecting U.S.

coastlines and harbors. Its members—both male and female—are called Coast Guardsmen. Right after the attack in New York City, Coast Guardsmen kept ships from leaving or entering New York Harbor, in case any of the ships held more terrorists. Coast Guardsmen closed off the Statue of Liberty, on Liberty Island in the harbor. They worried that it, too, might be a target. They guarded the many bridges that cross New York City's rivers. Coast Guard boats and aircraft also helped carry injured New Yorkers to safety.

Coast Guardsmen in other coastal cities took similar steps that day. In doing this work, the Coast Guard was continuing a long tradition of protecting U.S. waters.

The Coast Guard watched over the Brooklyn Bridge in New York City
in the days following the September 11, 2001, terrorist attacks.

A Coast Guard Defender Class Response boat patrols for safety and security. Defender Class boats replaced nearly 300 older boats as a result of standards established after September 11, 2001.

PATROLLING THE COASTS

The U.S. Coast Guard, a branch of the U.S. military, has many jobs. It operates search-and-rescue missions, looking for people whose boats or planes have been lost at sea. It helps boaters travel safely by providing warning signals, safety information, and weather reports. It helps keep people safe during natural disasters at sea, such as hurricanes. The Coast Guard also stops boats that are operating illegally. The boats might be unsafe. Or they might be carrying illegal goods, such as drugs. The Coast Guard tries to keep illegal immigrants from entering the country by boat. It also tries to keep criminals from leaving the country by boat. It breaks up ice on waterways to help keep boat traffic moving freely. It also helps the U.S. Navy during wartime. Finally, the

Coast Guard helps with homeland security—protecting the United States from terrorist attacks.

"If you want to boat, boat with the best."
–Coast Guard slogan

To do this work, the Coast Guard has bases on all U.S. shores, including the Atlantic Ocean, the Pacific Ocean, the Gulf of Mexico, and the Great Lakes. It patrols and protects this vast area with ships, boats, airplanes, and helicopters. It has approximately 39,000 full-time members, 1,400 boats, and 200 aircraft. The Coast Guard is headquartered in Washington, D.C.

A Coast Guard cutter cruises in front of U.S. Coast Guard headquarters in Washington, D.C.

THE EARLY YEARS

The U.S. Coast Guard has a long history, starting with the Revenue Cutter Service. The service was established on August 4, 1790, not long after the United States became an independent nation. The Revenue Cutter Service was part of the U.S. Treasury Department. The Treasury made foreign ships pay tariffs, or taxes, when they brought goods into the United States. It built 10 fast sailing ships, called cutters, to chase down ships that didn't pay the tariffs.

In 1794 the U.S. government gave the Revenue Cutter Service a new responsibility—stopping slave ships from entering the country. In 1797 the U.S. Congress passed a law saying that, if needed, Revenue Cutter Service ships could serve as fighting ships during war.

Slave ships carried hundreds of Africans in cramped quarters. One of the Revenue Cutter Service's early responsibilities was to stop slave ships from landing on U.S. shorelines.

A U.S. ship and a British ship battle during the War of 1812.

Along with the U.S. Navy and U.S. Army, the Revenue Cutter Service fought against the British in the War of 1812 (1812–1815). Using guns, swords, and cannons, cutter crews fought Britain's Royal Navy in the Atlantic Ocean. A cutter seized the first British ship to be captured during the war. Later, cutters were involved in some of the war's fiercest battles.

During the early 1800s, pirates prowled the Caribbean Sea, southeast of the United States. Pirate ships frequently attacked merchant (commercial) ships, killed their crews, and stole their supplies and cargo, including gold and silver. Pirates built hideouts around the Gulf of Mexico, especially along the Louisiana and Florida coasts. Sometimes they raided small coastal towns. Revenue Cutter Service crews fought against pirates whenever they found them.

The U.S revenue cutter *Alabama (above)* was attacked by
pirates off the coast of Florida in 1819.

On August 31, 1819, the pirate ship *Bravo* attacked
the cutters *Alabama* and *Louisiana* off the coast of
Florida. After firing on the *Bravo* with cannons, Cutter
Service crews boarded the *Bravo,* defeating the pirates
in hand-to-hand combat. The crews of the two cutters
then defeated other pirates on the Breton Islands near
New Orleans.

During the Second Seminole War (1835–1842), a
war fought against a Native American tribe called the
Seminoles, eight revenue cutters helped the army and
navy. The cutters blocked rivers to stop the movement
of Seminole troops and supplies. The cutters rescued
whites who had survived Seminole raids and helped
the army attack Seminole warriors. Cutter servicemen
fought with swords, muskets, rifles, and double-
barrel shotguns. During the Mexican-American War
(1846–1848), cutters helped the navy attack Mexico's
Atlantic and Pacific coasts.

In 1861 disagreement about slavery split the United States in two: North and South. The two sides fought a bitter war. The North won after four years of fighting. The Revenue Cutter Service assisted the U.S. Navy during the war, fighting for the North. Cutters patrolled U.S. waters, looking for enemy ships. Cutters also served as supply ships, carrying food and ammunition to the Northern army.

CHANGING ROLES

In 1878 the U.S. government created the U.S. Life-Saving Service to help boaters on U.S. waters. This new service rescued passengers of ships that had been wrecked or were sinking. In 1915 the Revenue Cutter Service and the U.S. Life-Saving Service were combined into one organization—the U.S. Coast Guard.

The U.S. Life-Saving Service responds to the distress signal of a ship out at sea.

The new organization took on a new job: patrolling the North Atlantic Ocean for icebergs. Ships that struck icebergs, such as the *Titanic* in 1912, were in danger of sinking. The Coast Guard's new Ice Patrol helped prevent such tragedies by tracking icebergs and telling ships how to steer clear of them.

During World War I (1914–1918), Coast Guard cutters were stationed in the North Atlantic Ocean and around Great Britain. They rescued British ships that were damaged or sinking after German submarine attacks. A German submarine sank the U.S. cutter *Tampa* off the coast of Wales on September 26, 1918. All of the Coast Guardsmen onboard were killed.

In 1920 Prohibition began in the United States. During this era, which lasted until 1933, selling

CUTTERS

The first Revenue Cutter Service cutters were 60 feet long, made of wood, and operated on wind power (using sails). They were equipped with big artillery pieces, such as cannons. In 1840 the Revenue Cutter Service began using steam-powered cutters. One cutter that fought during the Civil War (1861–1865) was part submarine, part boat. It normally traveled above the water. But to avoid attack, the cutter could run almost completely under the water.

By the late 1800s, cutters were made of steel instead of wood. By the early 1900s, cutters had diesel engines. During World War II (1939–1945), cutters were outfitted with new equipment. They used antiaircraft guns to fire at enemy airplanes. They used sonar and radar systems to detect enemy vehicles underwater, on land, and in the air.

Modern cutters are equipped with an antiaircraft weapon called the Phalanx Close-In Weapons System. This system combines radar and computer technology to locate and shoot down enemy aircraft and missiles. The system can shoot down the fastest missile in the thickest fog.

liquor was illegal. But many people broke the law. They smuggled liquor into the United States from Canada and from other countries. The Coast Guard's job was to stop smugglers from sneaking liquor into the country by boat. Coast Guardsmen chased smugglers along the Atlantic coast and on rivers and lakes separating the United States and Canada.

In 1928 the Coast Guard began using a new tool—airplanes—in its search-and-rescue missions. The Coast Guard used a special kind of airplane called a seaplane. This plane could land on and take off from water. Arriving by seaplane at the sight of a boat accident, Coast Guardsmen could jump into the water and rescue survivors.

The Coast Guard started using seaplanes for patrolling and for rescue missions in 1928. This seaplane floats in the water at Port Angeles, Washington, in the late 1930s.

Icebreaking service began in 1936. This U.S. Coast Guard icebreaker was photographed in 1952 in the Arctic Ocean.

In 1936 the Coast Guard began an icebreaking service. It used large ships known as icebreakers to crack through ice on northern waters, including the North Atlantic Ocean, the Great Lakes, and the Saint Lawrence River. Without icebreakers, ships could not travel freely along these waters in winter.

In 1939 the U.S. Lighthouse Service (formed in the late 1700s) became part of the Coast Guard. The agency operated lighthouses and lightships—ships equipped with powerful spotlights. Lighthouses and lightships helped guide boaters safely to and from U.S. shores.

BACK TO WAR

World War II (1939–1945) was fought in Europe, North Africa, and the Pacific Ocean. The United States entered the fighting in 1941. During the war, the Coast Guard patrolled U.S. coasts for enemy planes and ships. It carried navy troops and supplies across the oceans. Coast Guard boats carried troops from ship to shore during invasions. The Coast Guard also looked for and rescued U.S. pilots shot down over the water. Enemy ships and submarines often attacked Coast Guard ships. About 600 Coast Guardsmen died in combat during World War II, and many more were wounded.

Ships staffed by Coast Guardsmen unload troops in the surf on a beach in the Philippines in 1944.

During the Korean War (1950–1953), the United States fought alongside South Korea against North Korea. The Coast Guard went into action again. Retired Coast Guard officers helped train South Korean navy officers. The Coast Guard protected U.S. cargo ships and rescued navy ships that had been damaged by enemy fire. In the 1960s and early 1970s, the United States fought in the Vietnam War (1954–1975) in Southeast Asia. The Coast Guard patrolled the Vietnamese coast during this war, looking for enemy ships and assisting the U.S. Army, Navy, and Air Force.

The United States fought the Persian Gulf War (1991) against Iraq. During this war, the Coast Guard patrolled the Persian Gulf in the Middle East, preventing

The U.S. Coast Guard helped clean up the oil pollution in Kuwait after the Persian Gulf War in 1991.

supply ships from reaching the Iraqi army. When Iraq
released oil into the gulf, the Coast Guard helped clean
up the pollution. After the war was over, the Coast
Guard helped repair damaged oil wells and oil pumping
stations in the waters off Kuwait, Iraq's neighbor.

GUARDS OF THE HARBOR

After the terrorist attacks of September 11, 2001, the
Coast Guard worked
even harder to protect
U.S. harbors and
waterways. In the
weeks after the
attacks, the Coast
Guard tested the air in
New York City. It
helped find out how
much pollution had
been caused by fires,
dust, and dirt from the
collapsed World Trade
Center. The Coast
Guard also checked
suspicious boats in
New York Harbor for
terrorists.

President George W. Bush
established the Department of
Homeland Security in 2003.

In 2003 President George W. Bush established the
Department of Homeland Security to help protect the
United States from future terrorist attacks. The Coast
Guard became part of this new department. It took on
additional jobs, including patrolling and inspecting

places along the coast where terrorists might strike. It put up signs along waterways, telling people to look out for suspicious activities.

Also in 2003, the United States again went to war in Iraq. The Coast Guard played an important role in this war. It continues to work along with the U.S. Navy, patrolling waters near Iraq, looking for enemy ships and weapons. It guards ports in Iraq and makes sure that U.S. ships can safely carry weapons, supplies, and food to the nation.

chapter TWO

RECRUITMENT

EVERY YEAR, 4,000 new members enlist in, or join, the U.S. Coast Guard. Most of them are people who love boats and working on or near water. Newly enlisted members of the Coast Guard are called recruits.

High school students who are thinking about joining the Coast Guard might want to talk to a high school counselor. After that, the next step is to contact a local Coast Guard recruiter. Many cities have Coast Guard recruiting offices. The recruiters who work there can answer any questions a potential recruit might have.

To enlist in the Coast Guard, a recruit must be a U.S. citizen or a resident alien (a citizen of another country living legally in the United States). He or she must also have a high school diploma and be between 17 and 27 years old. But 17-year-olds need a parent's consent to join the Coast Guard.

After enlisting, recruits take a medical exam to make sure that they are in good health. They also take a test called the Armed Services Vocational Aptitude Battery (ASVAB). This multiple-choice test measures a recruit's math, language, science, electronics, and automotive skills. The test helps the Coast Guard determine which job recruits are best suited for. The Coast Guard tries to

New recruits stand in line. They must pass medical exams, written tests, and basic training to become members of the U.S. Coast Guard.

Some Coast Guard recruits are trained to work as firefighters.

give each recruit a job he or she wants. Sometimes, however, the Coast Guard assigns people to jobs it needs to fill. Some typical Coast Guard jobs are aviation mechanic, electrician, and food service specialist.

Recruits must sign a contract, promising to serve in the Coast Guard for at least four years. In return, the Coast Guard offers recruits pay and benefits. Starting pay for a recruit is about $1,000 per month. In addition to pay, the Coast Guard gives Coast Guardsmen food, housing, paid vacations, job training, health care, and life insurance. The Coast Guard also helps Coast Guardsmen pay for college.

Some people stay in the Coast Guard for more than four years. When their enlistment contracts expire, they "re-up," or sign up for another term of service. Some people spend their entire careers with the Coast Guard. After 20 years, they can retire with a pension (a monthly payment and health care benefits).

UNIFORMS

COAST GUARDSMEN WEAR several different uniforms. These uniforms are designed for different occasions and different kinds of weather.

WORKING BLUES

Coast Guardsmen usually wear working blues *(left)* when they're on the job. This uniform includes a baseball-style cap, a dark blue shirt, blue trousers, and boating shoes. In wet weather and on rough seas, Coast Guardsmen may also wear a parka. In cold weather, they may wear special gear that keeps them warm and dry.

UNDRESS BLUES

Undress blues—officially known as the operational dress uniform, or ODU—consist of trousers, a tie, a cap, and a short-sleeve shirt. Undress blues are worn in the field, where a more formal uniform isn't practical.

DRESS BLUES

Dress blues *(left)* are the standard uniform for formal Coast Guard occasions and ceremonies. This uniform has a dark blue suit coat and trousers, a light blue shirt, a tie, and a cap with a round brim. Tropical dress blues, for warm weather, have no dress coat and a short-sleeved shirt.

U.S. Coast Guard Song:
"Semper Paratus (Always Ready)"

From North and South and East and West,
The Coast Guard's in the fight.
Destroying subs and landing troops,
The Axis feels our might.
For we're the first invaders,
On every fighting field.
Afloat, ashore, on men and Spars,
You'll find the Coast Guard shield.

We're always ready for the call,
We place our trust in Thee.
Through howling gale and shot and shell,
To win our victory.
"Semper Paratus" is our guide,
Our pledge, our motto, too.
We're "Always Ready," do or die!
Aye! Coast Guard, we fight for you.

COAST GUARD RESERVE

Not all members of the Coast Guard are full-time Coast Guardsmen. Some people join a force called the U.S. Coast Guard Reserve. Members of the Coast Guard Reserve work part-time. They train one weekend per month and two weeks every summer. The rest of the time, they work in civilian (nonmilitary) jobs or attend school. During an emergency, reserves can be called into full-time, active duty. This happened after the September 11, 2001, terrorist attacks. To join, reservists must meet the same requirements as active-duty Coast Guardsmen. They also go through the same basic training.

The Coast Guard Selected Reserve has about 8,000 members.

Members of the Coast Guard Reserve were sent to patrol the waters of Boston Harbor in Massachusetts after the terrorist attacks on New York and Washington, D.C., in 2001.

This class taught by the Coast Guard Auxiliary shows kids how to properly use life jackets.

COAST GUARD AUXILIARY

The Coast Guard has another section called the U.S. Coast Guard Auxiliary, nicknamed America's Volunteer Lifesavers. Formed in 1939, this force has grown to include 35,000 members. They work as volunteers, meaning they don't get paid. They are also civilians.

After receiving special training, auxiliary members help the Coast Guard in many duties. They teach boating safety classes, carry out search-and-rescue missions, help prevent illegal fishing, and help stop the illegal dumping of wastes into U.S. waterways. Every year, members of the Coast Guard Auxiliary save more than 400 lives, assist almost 13,000 people (mostly boaters in distress), and teach almost 7,000 boating safety classes for children and adults.

WOMEN IN THE COAST GUARD

During the 1800s, women were not allowed to serve in the Revenue Cutter Service or in the U.S. Life-Saving Service. However, many women served in the U.S. Lighthouse Service. They worked as lighthouse keepers, or operators. When the Coast Guard was formed in 1915, women were not allowed to join the new organization.

In 1942, during World War II, the Coast Guard created a women's unit. The unit was nicknamed SPARS, which stands for Semper Paratus, Always Ready—the Coast Guard motto. The SPARS took over office jobs for male Coast Guardsmen, freeing up men to serve at sea. The SPARS ended after the war but started up again in 1949.

Women became full-time members of the Coast Guard in 1974. In 1976 the Coast Guard Academy became the first U.S. military academy to admit women. Other branches of the U.S. military don't allow women to hold certain jobs, such as combat jobs (jobs that involve fighting). But women in the Coast Guard can serve in any job.

Membership in the auxiliary is open to all U.S. citizens who are at least 17 years old. Many members are former active-duty Coast Guardsmen. Others are boaters who want to help other boaters and help keep U.S. waterways safe. The auxiliary works closely with the Coast Guard headquarters.

COAST GUARD OFFICERS

The senior leaders in the Coast Guard are called officers. They make important decisions and tell other Coast Guardsmen what to do.

Sometimes, Coast Guardsmen with professional experience, such as doctors or lawyers, are promoted to the officer ranks because the Coast Guard needs their skills. But most Coast Guardsmen become officers by enrolling in a special officer-training program. One program is the Coast Guard Academy, a four-year college. Another program is Officer Candidate School. This school provides advanced training for Coast Guardsmen who already have a college degree. Both schools are in New London, Connecticut.

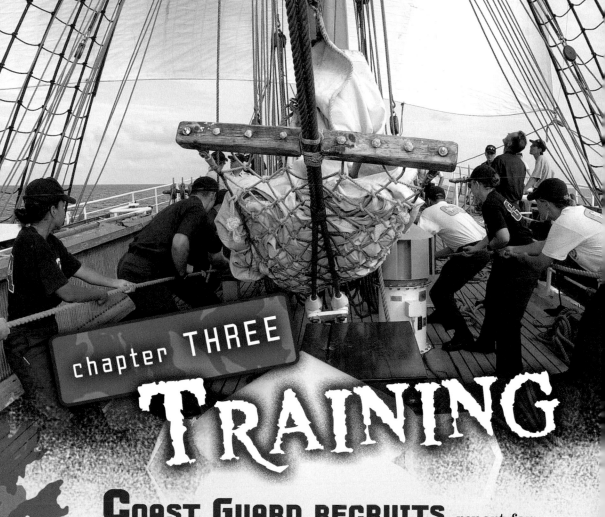

chapter THREE
TRAINING

COAST GUARD RECRUITS report for basic training, also called recruit training, at the U.S. Coast Guard Training Center in Cape May, New Jersey. Basic training is an eight-week program that teaches recruits how to be Coast Guardsmen.

During the first three days at training, recruits take medical exams and fill out lots of forms. They also receive a short haircut (shorter for men than women). The Coast Guard supplies recruits with everything they need for training, including uniforms. The only things recruits must bring with them to training are socks,

A new Coast Guard recruit receives a short haircut when he arrives for basic training.

underwear, and toilet items, such as shavers and toothbrushes.

Each recruit is assigned to a company, a group of between 100 and 150 men and women who will train together for the entire eight weeks. The officer in charge is called the company commander. He or she is the absolute boss during recruit training.

Recruits must follow the company commander's orders precisely.

RECRUIT TRAINING

The Coast Guard training program is tough. Monday through Saturday, recruits get up at 5:30 in the morning and go to bed at 9:00 at night. In between they attend classes, study, and do homework. Their lessons take place in the classroom, in swimming pools and gyms, and on boats on the water. Men and women train together in recruit training, but they live in separate barracks, or group housing facilities.

Female Coast Guard recruits stand at attention in their barracks.

During the first week, recruits learn about Coast Guard rules. They learn how to wear their uniforms correctly and how to treat Coast Guardsmen of a higher rank, such as officers. They learn to take orders—no questions asked. The most important lesson recruits learn during the first week of training is how to get along with others and to work as a team.

In the second week, recruits learn the Coast Guard chain of command, or who takes orders from whom. In the third week, they learn about the history of the Coast Guard and how to fire weapons. During the fourth week, they learn to identify different ships, boats, and airplanes. They take a midterm exam after week four.

A Coast Guard recruit learns how to fire a 9-millimeter pistol at a shooting range as part of basic training.

Water safety is an important part of Coast Guard training.

Then comes the fifth week, when recruits move out to boats on the water. There, they learn how to react in different emergencies. They learn how to avoid being washed overboard during a storm at sea, how to survive on an overturned boat, and how to treat injuries that might occur on a boat. In the sixth week, recruits learn how to put out a fire on a boat. In week seven, they learn how to dock and launch boats using heavy ropes called lines. Week eight features first aid lessons and lifesaving instruction in a swimming pool.

In addition to lessons in the classroom and on boats, recruits do a great deal of physical training. In the gym, recruits run laps and do calisthenics. In

Recruits must pass written and physical
tests to become Coast Guardsmen.

the pool, recruits learn the proper way to swim
using the freestyle stroke, breaststroke, butterfly
stroke, and backstroke.

Finally, recruits take a final exam, both physical and
written. They are tested on what they have learned in
the classroom. They must also pass a fitness test that
includes push-ups, sit-ups, running, and swimming.
They must be able to tread water for at least five
minutes. Those who pass the tests are no longer called
recruits. They are called Coast Guardsmen.

JOB TRAINING

After basic training, Coast Guardsmen get one or
two weeks leave (vacation). Then, some Coast

SINK OR SWIM

Serving in the Coast Guard is physically challenging work. Coast Guardsmen often work outdoors in bad weather and rough seas. To prepare for such a tough job, it helps to be in top condition when you enlist in the Coast Guard. It also helps to know how to swim.

Guardsmen travel to special stations to train for specific Coast Guard jobs. For instance, some Coast Guardsmen who will be working on cutters train at the U.S. Coast Guard Training Center in Yorktown, Virginia. Other Coast Guardsmen report right to their units after basic training. There, they attend special job training sessions and receive on-the-job training. Some learn to be mechanics, while others learn to be electricians. The training depends on the job.

At the Yorktown training center in Virginia, Coast Guardsmen practice using small raider boats outfitted with machine guns.

TOOLS OF THE TRADE

COAST GUARDSMEN USE A VARIETY OF TOOLS and vehicles in their work. This equipment includes watercraft (boats) such as cutters, aircraft such as helicopters, and communications systems such as radar and satellites.

WATERCRAFT

Icebreakers are 400-foot-long cutters with powerful engines. These cutters break up thick slabs of ice by slamming into them with their pointed bows (front ends). Motor lifeboats *(left)* are hard to sink. If this kind of boat tips over, it flips right side up again on its own. It automatically pumps out any water that might leak into it. The Coast Guard uses this kind of boat for search-and-rescue missions and for law enforcement.

AIRCRAFT

The HU-25 Falcon *(below)* is a small airplane that is used for surveillance (keeping watch). It can fly very low over the ground or water, enabling Coast Guardsmen to see objects below. The C-130 Hercules is a propeller plane that can carry a large amount of weight. It is used to carry supplies and equipment from one place to another. The HH-65A Dolphin *(right)* is a 44-foot-long helicopter. Coast Guardsmen use this helicopter to rescue people from

the water using a line and a harness or a basket. The MH-68A Stingray is a helicopter equipped with machine guns and rifles. It is used to fight drug smugglers and, if necessary, terrorists. Sharpshooters riding in the helicopter can fire on boats below.

COMMUNICATIONS EQUIPMENT

Radar is a system that sends out radio waves, which hit objects such as boats and airplanes and then bounce back. The returning signals tell radar operators where the objects are, how big they are, how fast they are going, and in what direction. Radar can even track rainstorms and other weather patterns.

Sonar is much like radar. This system uses sound waves to locate objects below the surface of the water. The Coast Guard uses sonar to locate vessels such as submarines and to identify underwater dangers such as rocks and reefs.

The Coast Guard uses satellites (space vehicles that orbit the earth) to locate distant objects on water. Satellites *(satellite dish left)* also track storms such as hurricanes.

The Coast Guard Academy is located in New London, Connecticut.

OFFICER TRAINING

Many Coast Guard officers train at the Coast Guard Academy, a four-year college in New London, Connecticut. Applicants must be U.S. citizens or resident aliens. They must be unmarried and between the ages of 17 and 23. Only those with good grades in high school will be admitted to the Coast Guard Academy.

Students at the academy are called cadets. Cadets take the same courses that many college students take: mathematics, engineering, computer classes, and communications classes, for example. They also take classes specific to serving in the Coast Guard, such as courses on ship design, ocean ecology, and meteorology (the study of weather). They might also study military history and tactics, and ways of fighting terrorism. Graduates receive a bachelor's degree and enter the Coast Guard with the officer rank of ensign. They must stay in the Coast Guard for at least five years.

Other officers train at the Coast Guard's Officer Candidate School, also in New London, Connecticut. Applicants to this program must already have a four-year college degree. Students at the school learn leadership skills, such as how and when to give orders, how to maintain discipline, and how to get the best out of the people they are commanding. They take classes on land (in the classroom) as well as on Coast Guard cutters and in aircraft. These classes might include navigation,

Students who graduate from the Coast Guard Academy become officers in the Coast Guard.

management, mathematics, flight training, and foreign languages. The training program is difficult and lasts only 17 weeks. Graduates enter the Coast Guard as ensigns and must serve for at least three years.

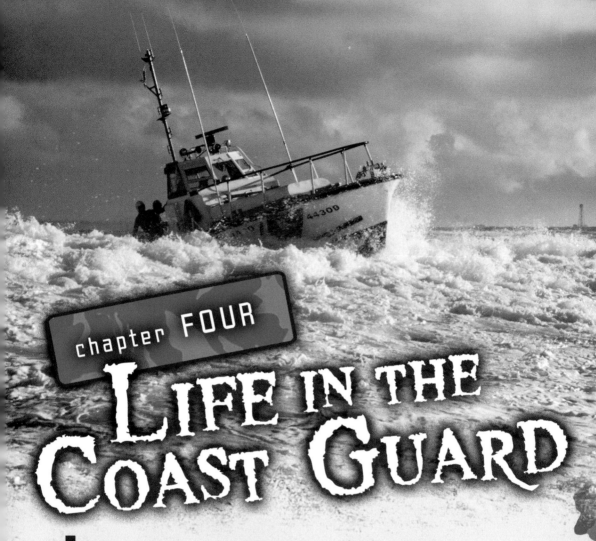

chapter FOUR
LIFE IN THE COAST GUARD

LIFE IN THE COAST GUARD can be
exciting. For instance, in July 2003, Hurricane Claudette
slammed into the coast of Texas, bringing with it 80-
mile-per-hour winds, eight inches of rain, and tides six
feet above normal. The storm damaged more than 100
miles of coastline. Houses collapsed. Power went out.
But no one was killed or hurt.

Why not? In large part, because the Coast Guard
was there to help. Before the storm struck, Coast
Guardsmen helped people living near the beach move
inland. After the storm struck, Coast Guardsmen

helped rescue people who had stayed in their homes from dangerous floodwaters. Coast Guardsmen also rescued people caught at sea in boats.

Not every day in the life of a seaman is as exciting as the day Hurricane Claudette hit Texas, however. Some days are very routine. And a Coast Guardman's day-to-day life depends a lot on his or her job and station.

JOBS IN THE COAST GUARD

The Coast Guard needs people to perform many different jobs. It needs people to operate computers and people to repair airplanes. It needs flight managers to make sure that aircraft take off and land on schedule.

Coast Guard maintenance crews inspect
and repair a rescue helicopter.

Many people in the Coast Guard work on cutters. These Coast Guardsmen include damage controllers (Coast Guardsmen who know how to put out fires on boats and to make repairs using welders and other machines). Gunner's mates are Coast Guardsmen who know how to clean, repair, load, and fire a ship's guns. Other Coast Guardsmen know how to use cranes to load and unload cargo and how to handle the cutters' many lines.

A drug-sniffing dog helps a member of the Coast Guard inspect a boat for illegal substances.

Coast Guard bands play at ceremonies and celebrations.

The Coast Guard also includes criminal investigators who work on antismuggling and antiterror missions. These Coast Guardsmen stop and search suspicious boats for illegal weapons and illegal goods.

The Coast Guard also needs musicians (who play at Coast Guard ceremonies and special occasions), storekeepers, and electricians. Everyone has to eat, so the Coast Guard always needs cooks, called food service specialists. People who join the Coast Guard have dozens of jobs to choose from. The Coast Guard tries to match each recruit with the right job.

This Coast Guard base in Florida is just one of almost 1,000 Coast Guard stations around the country.

COAST GUARD STATIONS

The Coast Guard has almost 1,000 stations in the United States and about 10 stations in other countries. All Coast Guard stations are near water. Most stations are by the ocean, but some are found along major rivers or lakes. Many stations are based on large Coast Guard cutters. Most Coast Guard stations share land and buildings with other government organizations, such as other branches of the U.S. military or the National Park Service.

Coast Guard stations vary in size and setup. Stations on large cutters usually include offices, dining areas, and barracks where Coast Guardsmen sleep. Stations on small cutters might not have barracks. The Coast Guardsmen

THE COAST GUARD DEDICATION

Every recruit is expected to memorize the "Coast Guard Dedication." It goes like this:

Honor. Absolute integrity is our standard. A Coast Guard member demonstrates honor in all things: never lying, cheating, or stealing. We do the right thing because it is the right thing—all the time.

Respect. We value the dignity and worth of people: whether a stranded boater, an immigrant, or a fellow Coast Guard member; we honor, protect, and assist.

Devotion to Duty. A Coast Guard member is dedicated to five maritime [sea-related] security roles: Maritime Safety, Maritime Law Enforcement, Marine Environmental Protection, Maritime Mobility, and National Defense. We are loyal and accountable to the public trust. We welcome responsibility.

who work there have to sleep at another nearby station or at a nearby apartment. Stations on land also vary, depending on the kind of work that goes on there. For instance, Coast Guard air stations have airports. Some stations have medical clinics, where Coast Guardsmen can give first aid treatment to injured boaters.

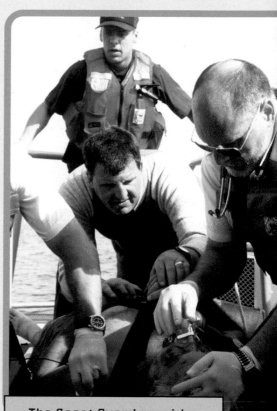

The Coast Guard provides emergency medical attention to injured boaters.

INSIGNIA

EVERYONE IN THE COAST GUARD has a rank—
a place in the chain of command. Coast Guardsmen
start out with the lowest rank—seaman recruit—when
they enlist in the Coast Guard. If seamen recruits do
what they are told and do it well, they will be
promoted to a higher rank. They will get more pay
and more responsibilities.

The first promotion usually comes when recruits
complete basic training. They become seamen apprentices.
Each rank comes with a different insignia, or symbol, that
Coast Guardsmen sew onto their uniforms. Here's a chart of
Coast Guard ranks and insignia from lowest to highest.

ENLISTED SEAMEN

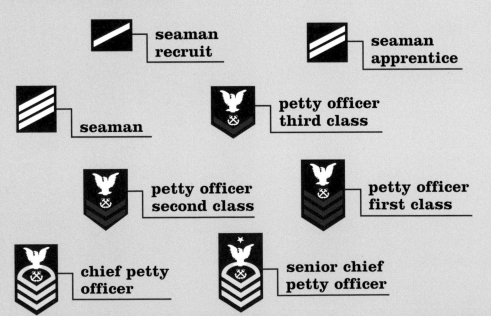

seaman
recruit

seaman
apprentice

seaman

petty officer
third class

petty officer
second class

petty officer
first class

chief petty
officer

senior chief
petty officer

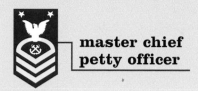 master chief
petty officer

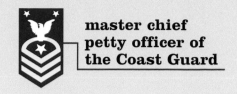 master chief
petty officer of
the Coast Guard

OFFICERS

ensign

lieutenant
junior grade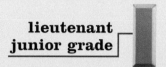

lieutenant

lieutenant
commander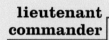

commander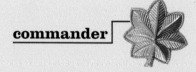

captain

rear admiral
(lower half)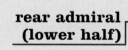

rear admiral
(upper half)

vice admiral

admiral

A TYPICAL DAY

A Coast Guardman's typical day depends on his or her job. Some Coast Guardsmen live on 180-foot ships called buoy tenders. They may live on these ships for six months at a time. They sometimes work a 24-hour shift, with every other day off. When the ship is in dock, the Coast Guardsmen can go onshore, walking across a large gangplank to the pier.

The Coast Guardsmen sleep in bunks called a stack, with three beds stacked up on top of one another. The workday begins at 6:00 A.M. The Coast Guardsmen have a quick breakfast in the ship's dining quarters, then go to work. As the ship prepares to get under way, the Coast Guardsmen load food and supplies and take garbage off the ship. They untie the lines that keep the ship attached to the pier. By 8:00 A.M., the ship is under way.

At sea the Coast Guardsmen place buoys, or floating markers. They use a large crane to lower

The Coast Guard maintains the buoys that help ships navigate in the ocean.

DANGEROUS WORK

During Hurricane Claudette in 2003, the Coast Guard made a daring rescue. Two men in a shrimp boat had decided to brave the storm. They found themselves in deep trouble once the winds and high waves struck. They managed to call the Coast Guard on their boat's radio. The Coast Guard sent a rescue helicopter to the scene. By the time the helicopter arrived, the boat had capsized and the men were clinging to its hull (body). From the helicopter, the Coast Guardsmen lowered ropes to the men and pulled them up, one at a time, to safety.

the buoys into the water. Some buoys mark spots where water is very shallow or where boats can get stuck in the mud or crash into a reef. Other buoys hold equipment that tracks the weather. These buoys have to be placed hundreds of miles out to sea.

In addition to placing buoys, the Coast Guardsmen check fishing boats to make sure the fishers have permits. They check suspicious boats for illegal drugs. They might even

A Coast Guardsman measures a fish on a fishing boat to make sure it is within the size allowed by the law.

Coast Guard helicopters and boats work together on search-and-rescue missions.

take part in a search-and-rescue mission, helping a damaged sailboat get ashore. In between, some Coast Guardsmen paint and clean the ship. The ship returns to shore in the evening. But some Coast Guardsmen might have to work all night, standing watch, maintaining the ship's equipment, or helping prepare for the next day's mission. Others will return to the stack for lights out at 10:00 P.M.

WAR AND TERRORISM

Most Coast Guard work does not involve fighting enemies. But the Coast Guard is a military organization. During times of war or terrorist attack, the Coast Guard must be ready to fight. Many Coast

GUN CONTROL

Only Coast Guardsmen specially trained in law enforcement—those who fight smugglers and terrorists—carry weapons. These weapons include handguns, shotguns, rifles, and machine guns. Cutters used for law enforcement have large machine guns mounted on their decks.

Guard ships and airplanes are equipped with state-of-the-art weapons. In wartime the Coast Guard works closely with the army, navy, air force, and marines.

Before September 11, 2001, only about 2 percent of Coast Guard missions involved protecting U.S. ports from enemy attacks. After September 11, that number jumped to 56 percent. Coast Guardsmen who once spent their time looking for drug smugglers or illegal immigrants began to search for terrorists, weapons, and explosives as well.

As part of the U.S. military, the Coast Guard is prepared to fight during wartime.

For many years, Coast Guard pilots have kept a lookout for planes carrying smuggled goods. Since September 11, the pilots must also look out for terrorists who might be planning an attack from the sky.

To fight terrorism, the Coast Guard works closely with other government agencies. For instance, the Coast Guard works with the U.S. Border Patrol to keep terrorists from getting into the United States. The Coast Guard works with the Federal Bureau of Investigation to search for terrorists who might already be living in the United States. The Coast Guard uses powerful computers to share information on terrorists with other government organizations.

The Coast Guard works together with the New York Police Department Harbor Unit to patrol New York Harbor.

The Coast Guard is always on the cutting edge with technology to improve search-and-rescue missions.

THE FUTURE OF THE COAST GUARD

What will the Coast Guard be like in the future? From its very start, the Coast Guard has been the nation's number-one search-and-rescue force along the shore. The Coast Guard will continue to find and rescue people in trouble at sea. The technology for this rescue work will improve.

Satellites hundreds of miles up in space will help the Coast Guard locate targets on earth—even targets as small as a person clinging to a piece of driftwood. Better satellites will predict the weather more accurately.

This U.S. Coast Guard cutter stands ready to support troops in the Persian Gulf region.

The Coast Guard will grow even better at keeping criminals off the water. Coast Guard aircraft and boats will be faster, with better equipment for detecting smugglers and terrorists. In short, no matter what the challenge—whether it's posed by nature, enemy troops, terrorists, or smugglers—the Coast Guard will be ready.

STRUCTURE

UNLIKE OTHER U.S. MILITARY BRANCHES, which are strictly divided into groups such as platoons, companies, and battalions, the Coast Guard is organized differently. Coast Guardsmen belong to small units such as boat stations, cutters, or aids to navigation teams. These units can vary in size from just a few people to a hundred people. These organizations belong to larger groups, or zones, which belong to one of nine Coast Guard districts. Each district is based in a different city around the United States. District commanders, usually holding the rank of admiral, report to the commandant of the Coast Guard, who reports to the secretary of homeland security, who works for the president of the United States.

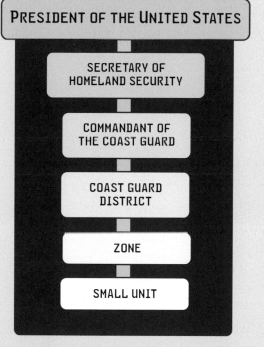

PRESIDENT OF THE UNITED STATES

SECRETARY OF HOMELAND SECURITY

COMMANDANT OF THE COAST GUARD

COAST GUARD DISTRICT

ZONE

SMALL UNIT

TIMELINE

1790 The Revenue Cutter Service is established.

1794 The Revenue Cutter Service begins to stop slave ships from entering the United States.

1812–1815 Revenue cutters fight against Great Britain's Royal Navy in the War of 1812.

1800–1820s Revenue cutters battle pirates in the Caribbean Sea.

1861–1865 Revenue cutters fight in the Civil War.

1878 The U.S. Life-Saving Service is formed.

1915 The Revenue Cutter Service and U.S. Life-Saving Service are combined into the U.S. Coast Guard.

1920 Prohibition begins. The Coast Guard stops people trying to smuggle liquor into the United States.

1928 The Coast Guard begins search-and-rescue missions by airplane.

1933 Prohibition ends.

1936 The Coast Guard begins an icebreaking service on northern waters.

1939 The U.S. Lighthouse Service becomes part of the U.S. Coast Guard.

1941–1945 The Coast Guard works alongside the navy during World War II.

1950–1953 The Coast Guard helps South Korea and the U.S. Navy during the Korean War.

1960s–1970s The Coast Guard prevents enemy ships from coming ashore in Vietnam during the Vietnam War.

1991 The Coast Guard guards the Persian Gulf during the Persian Gulf War.

2001 The Coast Guard protects New York Harbor after the September 11 terrorist attacks.

2003 The Coast Guard becomes part of the new Department of Homeland Security.

2003–2004 The Coast Guard assists the U.S. Navy and other military branches fighting the war in Iraq.

GLOSSARY

cutter: a Coast Guard boat longer than 60 feet

homeland security: the government's effort to protect the United States from terrorist and military attacks. The U.S. Coast Guard became part of the Department of Homeland Security in 2003.

icebreakers: ships designed to break up ice-filled waterways to prevent delays in boat traffic

lightships: ships equipped with powerful spotlights. Lightships were once used to guide other ships along U.S. coasts in areas where there were no lighthouses.

navigation: charting and directing the course of a vessel or aircraft to arrive at the correct destination

radar: a device that uses radio signals to determine the location of objects such as aircraft, boats, or storms

satellites: unmanned craft that circle the earth in space. Satellites often carry high-powered cameras and communications equipment.

seaplanes: airplanes that can land on and take off from water

search-and-rescue mission: a mission to look for people whose boat or plane has been lost at sea

sonar: a device that uses sound waves to locate objects underwater

surveillance: watching people or places, usually to spot illegal or enemy activity

terrorism: attacks to frighten or kill civilians rather than soldiers

FAMOUS PEOPLE

Al Barlick (1915–1995) Born in Springfield, Illinois, Barlick was a Major League Baseball umpire. He served in the Coast Guard during World War II. Known for his flashy calls, he worked for 33 years as a big-league ump. In 1989 he was elected into the National Baseball Hall of Fame.

Vivien S. Crea (born 1952) Rear Admiral Crea was born in Seoul, South Korea. After entering the Coast Guard as a pilot in 1973, she became the first female aircraft commander in the Coast Guard. In 2002 she became commander of the First Coast Guard District. In this position, she oversees all Coast Guard operations in the northeastern United States.

Buddy Ebsen (1908–2003) A TV and movie actor, Ebsen was born in Belleville, Illinois. He was best known for his roles in the long-running *Beverly Hillbillies* and *Barnaby Jones* TV shows. Ebsen served three years in the Coast Guard during World War II.

Alex Haley (1921–1992) Born in Ithaca, New York, Haley is most famous as the author of *Roots* (1976), a book that traces the history of an African American family. Haley served in the U.S. Coast Guard from 1939 to 1959. He began writing articles and short stories during his service. After retiring from the Coast Guard, Haley became a full-time writer. In 1999 the Coast Guard honored Haley by naming a cutter after him.

Betty Hicks (born 1921) After taking up golf at age 16, Hicks enlisted in the Coast Guard as a SPAR during World War II. She served until 1944, then became a pro golfer. A native of Long Beach, California, Hicks was a founding member of the Ladies Professional Golf Association (LPGA). She retired from tournament play after many wins and became a golf teacher. In 1999 the LPGA honored Hicks for her contribution to the early growth of the sport.

Andy Liebner (born 1983) A native of Kenai, Alaska, Liebner serves at a Coast Guard search-and-rescue station in Michigan. He is not famous yet, but he wants to be. Liebner hopes to compete as a member of the U.S. Olympic ski team in 2006. He specializes in the biathlon, an event that combines cross-country skiing and rifle sharpshooting.

G. William Miller (born 1925) Miller, a native of Sapulpa, Oklahoma, served as secretary of the U.S. Treasury from 1979 to 1981, during the presidency of Jimmy Carter. In 1945 he graduated from the U.S. Coast Guard Academy with a degree in marine engineering. He served until 1949, working as an officer in Asia and the United States.

Arnold Palmer (born 1929) Born in Latrobe, Pennsylvania, Palmer started playing golf at age three. In 1947 he entered Wake Forest University in North Carolina. He enlisted in the Coast Guard in 1950 and served until 1953. He returned to Wake Forest and in 1954 won golf's U.S. Amateur tournament. As a professional, he won four Masters tournaments, one U.S. Open, two British Opens, and two U.S. Senior Opens.

James Pollard (1922–1993) Born in Oakland, California, basketball player Pollard led Stanford University to a National Collegiate Athletic Association championship in 1942. He was nicknamed the Kangaroo Kid because he was a great jumper. Playing with the Minneapolis Lakers, Pollard won four National Basketball Association championships. Pollard served in the Coast Guard in the Pacific Ocean during World War II. He was inducted into the Basketball Hall of Fame in 1978.

Gene Taylor (born 1953) Born in New Orleans, Louisiana, Taylor is a U.S. congressperson representing the Bay Saint Louis area of Mississippi. A member of the House Armed Services Committee and the House Transportation and Infrastructure Committee, Taylor served in the Coast Guard Reserve from 1971 to 1984. From 1975 on, he worked as the skipper (leader) of a search-and-rescue boat.

BIBLIOGRAPHY

Baker, A. D. *The Naval Institute Guide to Combat Fleets of the World.* Annapolis, MD: Naval Institute Press, 2000.

Larzelere, Alex. *The Coast Guard at War: Vietnam, 1965–1975.* Annapolis, MD: Naval Institute Press, 1997.

Noble, Dennis L. *Lifeboat Sailors: Inside the Coast Guard's Small Boat Stations.* Washington, DC: Brassey's, 2000.

Scotti, Paul C. *Coast Guard Action in Vietnam: Stories of Those Who Served.* Central Point, OR: Hellgate Press, 2000.

Shanks, Ralph, and Wick York. *The U.S. Life-Saving Service: Heroes, Rescues and Architecture of the Early Coast Guard.* Petaluma, CA: Costano Books, 1996.

FURTHER READING

Donovan, Sandy. *Protecting America: A Look at the People Who Keep Our Country Safe.* Minneapolis: Lerner Publications Company, 2004.

Gaines, Ann Graham. *The Coast Guard in Action.* Berkeley Heights, NJ: Enslow Publishers, Inc., 2001.

Holden, Henry M. *Coast Guard Rescue and Patrol Aircraft.* Berkeley Heights, NJ: Enslow Publishers, Inc., 2002.

Lyons, Lewis, et al. *Rescue at Sea with the U.S. and Canadian Coast Guards.* Broomall, PA: Mason Crest, 2003.

Streissguth, Thomas. *The U.S. Navy.* Minneapolis: Lerner Publications Company, 2005.

Van Orden, M. D., and Arleigh A. Burke. *U.S. Navy Ships and Coast Guard Cutters.* Annapolis, MD: Naval Institute Press, 1990.

Weintraub, Aileen. *Life inside the Coast Guard.* San Francisco: Children's Book Press, 2002.

Williams, Barbara. *World War II: Pacific.* Minneapolis: Lerner Publications Company, 2005.

Zwier, Lawrence J., and Matthew S. Weltig. *The Persian Gulf and Iraqi Wars.* Minneapolis: Lerner Publications Company, 2005.

WEBSITES

Coast Guard Office of Boating Safety
<http://www.uscgboating.org/>
At this site, visitors learn how to prevent accidents, injuries, and deaths while boating. They can also review boating safety tips, news, and laws and regulations.

Today's Military
<http://www.todaysmilitary.com/wyg/t2_wyg_careers.php>
This website offers information for people interested in a career in the U.S. military, including the Coast Guard.

U.S. Coast Guard
<http://www.uscg.mil/>
The official website of the Coast Guard provides news and information about Coast Guard activities, the history of the Coast Guard, and jobs available to Coast Guardsmen.

U.S. Coast Guard Academy
<http://www.cga.edu/>
The U.S. Coast Guard Academy website contains information about the school, including information on classes, sports programs, cadet life, and the campus.

U.S. Coast Guard Auxiliary
<http://www.cgaux.org/>
This site discusses the various roles of the auxiliary, such as public education, vessel safety checks, safety patrols, search and rescue, maritime security, and environmental protection.

U.S. Coast Guard Navigation Center
<http://www.navcen.uscg.gov/>
This site provides information on Coast Guard satellite use, radio communication, navigation, and search-and-rescue missions.

U.S. Coast Guard: The Shield of Freedom
This is the recruiting site for the U.S. Coast Guard and U.S. Coast Guard Reserve, with information about Coast Guard jobs and careers, how to find a recruiter, and scholarship programs.

INDEX

ABOUT THE AUTHOR

Michael Benson is the former editor of the *Military Technical Journal.* He is also the author of 30 books, including *The Encyclopedia of the JFK Assassination* and several titles in the Complete Idiot's series. He has written biographies of Ronald Reagan, Bill Clinton, William Howard Taft, Malcolm X, Muhammad Ali, Dale Earnhardt, and Gloria Estefan. Originally from Rochester, New York, he is a graduate of Hofstra University. He lives with his wife and two children in Brooklyn, New York.

PHOTO ACKNOWLEDGMENTS

The images in this book are used with the permission of: The U.S. Coast Guard, pp. 4, 5, 6, 7, 11, 17, 19, 20, 21, 23, 25, 26, 27, 29, 30, 31, 32, 33, 34, 35, 36 (both), 37 (top), 38, 39, 41, 42, 43, 45 (both), 48, 49, 50, 51, 52, 53, 54; © North Wind Picture Archives, p. 8; National Archives, pp. 9 (W&C 079), 15 (W&C 1210); Library of Congress, p.10 [LC-USZ62-14103]; © Museum of Flight/CORBIS, p. 13; © Bettmann/CORBIS, p. 14; © Getty Images, p.16; © Reuters/CORBIS, p. 22; © Royalty-Free/CORBIS, p. 37 (bottom); © Jim Sugar/CORBIS, p. 40; © Art Seltz/ZUMA Press, p. 44; © Todd Strand/Independent Picture Service, p. 47 (officer insignias).

Cover image: © Reuters/CORBIS